ECDL Module 6:
Presentation

Springer
London
Berlin
Heidelberg
New York
Barcelona
Hong Kong
Milan
Paris
Singapore
Tokyo

ICDL Approved Courseware
Syllabus Version 3.0

ECDL Approved Courseware
Syllabus Version 3.0

ECDL Module 6: Presentation

ECDL – the European PC standard

by **David Stott**

The Publisher and the BCS would like to publicly acknowledge the vital support of the ECDL Foundation in validating and approving this book for the purpose of studying for the European-wide ECDL qualification.

Springer-Verlag London Ltd, Sweetapple House, Catteshall Road, Godalming, Surrey GU7 3DJ or

The British Computer Society, 1 Sanford Street, Swindon, Wiltshire SN1 1HJ

ISBN 1-85233-447-9

British Library Cataloguing in Publication Data

Stott, David
    ECDL module 6: presentation: ECDL – the European PC standard. – (European computer
    driving licence)
    1. Microsoft PowerPoint (Computer file) 2. Business presentations - Data processing
    I. Title
    006.6'869

    ISBN 1852334479

Printed and bound at The Cromwell Press, Trowbridge, Wiltshire, England.
34/3830-543210 Printed on acid-free paper SPIN 10792536

Preface

This book is intended to help you successfully complete the test for Module 6 of the European Computer Driving Licence (ECDL). However before we start working through the actual content of the guide you may find it useful to know a little bit more about the ECDL in general and where this particular Module fits into the overall framework.

What Is The ECDL?

The European Computer Driving Licence (ECDL) is a European-wide qualification that enables people to demonstrate their competence in computer skills. It certifies the candidate's knowledge and competence in personal computer usage at a basic level and is based upon a single agreed syllabus.

This syllabus covers a range of specific knowledge areas and skill sets, which are broken down into seven modules. Each of the modules must be passed before the ECDL certificate can be awarded, though they may be taken in any order but must be completed within a three year period.

Testing of candidates is at audited testing centres, and successful completion of the test will demonstrate the holder's basic knowledge and competence in using a personal computer and common computer applications.

The implementation of the ECDL in the UK is being managed by the British Computer Society. It is growing at a tremendous rate and is set to become the most widely recognised qualification in the field of work-related computer use.

The ECDL Modules

The seven modules which make up the ECDL certificate are described briefly below:

Module 1: Basic Concepts of Information Technology covers the physical make-up of a personal computer and some of the basic concepts of Information Technology such as data storage and memory, and the uses of information networks within computing. It also looks at the application of computer software in society and the use of IT systems in everyday situations. Some basic security and legal issues are also addressed.

Module 2: Using the Computer and Managing Files covers the basic functions of a personal computer and its operating system. In particular it looks at operating effectively within the desktop environment, managing and organising files and directories, and working with desktop icons.

Module 3: Word Processing covers the use of a word processing application on a personal computer. It looks at the basic operations associated with creating, formatting and finishing a word processing document ready for distribution. It also addresses some of the more advanced features such as creating standard tables, using pictures and images within a document, importing objects and using mail merge tools.

Module 4: Spreadsheets covers the basic concepts of spreadsheets and the ability to use a spreadsheet application on a personal computer. Included are the basic operations for developing, formatting and using a spreadsheet, together with the use of basic formulas and functions to carry out standard mathematical and logical operations. Importing objects and creating graphs and charts are also covered.

Module 5: Database covers the basic concepts of databases and the ability to use a database on a personal computer. It addresses the design and planning of a simple database, and the retrieval of information from a database through the use of query, select and sort tools.

Module 6: Presentation covers the use of presentation tools on a personal computer, in particular creating, formatting and preparing presentations. The requirement to create a variety of presentations for different audiences and situations is also addressed.

Module 7: Information and Communication is divided into two main sections, the first of which covers basic Web search tasks using a Web browser and search engine tools. The second section addresses the use of electronic mail software to send and receive messages, to attach documents, and to organise and manage message folders and directories.

This guide focuses upon Module 6.

How To Use This Guide

The purpose of this guide is to take you through all of the knowledge areas and skill sets specified in the syllabus for Module 6. The use of clear, non technical explanations and self paced exercises will provide you with an understanding of the key elements of the syllabus and give you a solid foundation for moving on to take the ECDL test relating to this Module. All exercises contained within this guide are based upon the Windows 98 operating system and Office 97 software.

Each chapter has a well defined set of objectives that relate directly to the syllabus for the ECDL Module 6. Because the guide is structured in a logical sequence you are advised to work through the chapters one at a time from the beginning. Throughout each chapter there are various review questions so that you can determine whether you have understood the principles involved correctly prior to moving on to the next step.

Conventions Used In This Guide

Throughout this guide you will come across notes alongside a number of icons. They are all designed to provide you with specific information related to the section of the book you are currently working through. The icons and the particular types of information they relate to are as follows:

Additional Information: Further information or explanation about a specific point.

Caution: A word of warning about the risks associated with a particular action, together with guidance, where necessary on how to avoid any pitfalls.

Definition: A plain English definition of a newly introduced term or concept.

Short Cuts: Short cuts and hints for using a particular program more effectively.

As you are working through the various exercises contained within this guide, you will be asked to carry out a variety of actions:

● Where we refer to commands or items that you are required to select from the PC screen, then we indicate these in bold, for example: Click on the **Yes** button.
● Where you are asked to key text in to the PC, then we indicate this in italics, for example: Type in the words '*Saving my work*'.

You should now be in a position to use this guide, so lets get started. Good luck!

Contents

Introduction

Module 6 of the ECDL qualification is concerned with the subject of Presentation applications and is based on Microsoft's PowerPoint 97 software.

Before embarking on the task of learning how to use PowerPoint it is important to understand what Presentation packages are and what role they play in modern PC based computing.

Presentation Graphics Software: The modern presentation graphics package is a tool that can be used to create, edit, modify, and display information in a structured and controlled manner as an aid to communication. We have all probably seen presentations using equipment like flip charts, white boards, or overhead projectors but a presentation graphics program allows you to utilise PC technology to deliver presentations effectively and professionally.

Like most other presentation graphics packages, PowerPoint is based on the "slide show" metaphor and in essence it can be used to produce "virtual" slides which can subsequently be displayed on the PC screen. However, PowerPoint is not solely designed for displaying slides on-screen and you can use the package to create actual 35mm slides via a bureau service, printed black and white or full colour overhead transparency sheets, speaker notes, audience handouts, and presentation outlines.

If you intend to use PowerPoint to create overhead transparency sheets make sure that you use the correct materials that are specifically designed for your printer. In particular, you MUST use film sheets that are guaranteed heat proof when using a laser printer.

Presentations can come in all shapes and sizes, both formal and informal and many organisations make extensive use of presentations as a method of providing effective communication of ideas, concepts or factual data. Typically, presentations may used as an adjunct to such as product marketing, product sales, training, education, committee or board meetings, and basically in any situation where a speaker needs to deliver information to an audience.

Microsoft PowerPoint 97 has some key features which make it suitable for generating a wide variety of presentations and we shall cover a number of these in this Module. Using PowerPoint you can perform the following tasks:

● Create, edit and save presentations.
● Modify existing presentations.
● Publish presentations on Internet web pages.
● Create slides containing text, images, audio, and video.
● Copy, move, delete, or rearrange slides or slide elements.
● Modify and format text and borders.
● Draw lines, boxes and other shapes on slides.
● Include organisation and other types of charts on slides.
● Incorporate information from other packages on slides.
● Print slides, presentation outlines, speaker notes, and audience handouts in various formats.
● Apply animation to various objects on slides.
● Set up special transitions between slides when displaying presentations.
● Control and navigate through onscreen Slide Shows.

This guide is structured in chapters that are designed to be followed in a logical sequence, therefore you are advised to work through the guide one chapter at a time from the beginning. At the end of each chapter there are some review questions so that you can determine whether or not you have understood the principles involved correctly. Throughout this guide the following conventions have been used:

Text	instructions for you to follow or things that you should type.
Click	single click of the mouse button (left button unless specifically stated).
Double Click	two successive clicks of the mouse button (assume left button only).
	toolbar icon or other window control which should be selected with the mouse.
F1	specific keyboard key which you should use.

Getting Started

In this chapter you will learn how to

- Open a new presentation application.

- Open an existing presentation document, make some modifications and save it.

- Open several different presentations at the same time

- Save an existing presentation onto the hard disk or a diskette.

- Use the application Help functions.

- Change the display modes.

- Use the page view magnification tool and zoom tool.

- Modify the toolbar display.

- Save an existing presentation under another file format.

- Save a presentation in a format appropriate for posting to a Web Site.

.

1.1. First Steps with Presentation Tools

Before we begin we need to check whether Microsoft PowerPoint is already installed on your PC. Click on the **Start** button and select the **Programs** option. You should see a list of installed programs, PowerPoint may be listed here or it may be under the Microsoft Office option, this depends on how you system has been setup, as in the example in Figure 1.1.

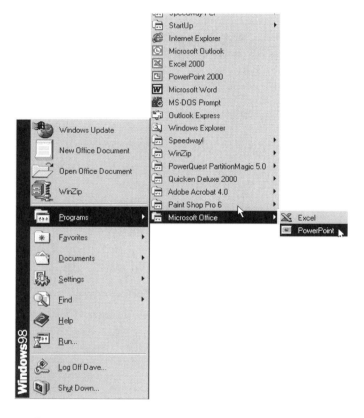

Figure 1.1 Starting PowerPoint from the Start button.

Note that there may be other Microsoft Office programs also installed on your PC, such as, Word, Access, or Excel. However, it should be fairly obvious whether PowerPoint is installed or not.

If Microsoft PowerPoint is not already installed on your PC
you should follow the instructions for setting up the
software as detailed in the Office 97 "Getting Started"
guide. These instructions are quite straightforward but if
you have any difficulty installing the software then seek
advice from your computer supplier or system
administrator.

Assuming that PowerPoint is installed on your PC we are now ready to
start learning how to use it to create and edit presentations.
PowerPoint is an extremely flexible package and can be used to create
a wide variety of different presentations for different purposes. Your
PowerPoint presentations can be as simple or as complicated as you
like and you will soon learn how to create basic presentations that can
be enhanced to produce interesting and dynamic looking slide shows.

In this initial section we will look at the following basic procedures:

● Open a presentation application.
● Open an existing presentation document – make some modifications
  and save.
● Open several documents.
● Save an existing presentation onto the hard disk or a diskette.
● Close the presentation document.
● Use application Help functions.

Exercise 1.1

In this exercise we will look at what happens when you start PowerPoint and
how to proceed to open, close and save presentations. We will also look at
how PowerPoint can provide Help if and when you get stuck.

1. Open PowerPoint by selecting it from the **Start I Programs** option on the
Task Bar as in the example in Figure 1.1.

Each time you start the PowerPoint program you will see the dialogue box as
in Figure 1.2.

11

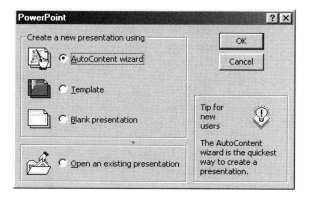

Figure 1.2 Dialogue box displayed when PowerPoint is started.

Here you have the choice of creating a new presentation or opening an existing presentation.

2. For the moment we will ignore the creation of new presentations so you need to select **Open an existing presentation** and click on **OK**.

The **Open File** dialogue box should appear and by default the folder **My Documents** is displayed, as in Figure 1.3.

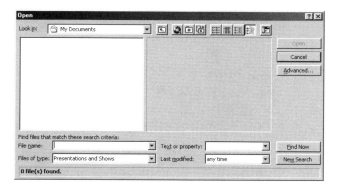

Figure 1.3 The Open File dialogue box showing the My Documents folder.

Don't be alarmed if there are no presentations displayed for you to open. The chances are that if this is the first time you have run PowerPoint there will be no presentations in the **My Documents** folder so we will need to look somewhere else to find some existing presentations to open.

3. Using the **Look in:** drop down list select **C:\Windows\Program Files\ Office 97\Office** folder. Once selected you should see an entry called **Ppcentrl.pps** and you should now select this and click on the **Open** button. You should now see a warning message as in Figure 1.4.

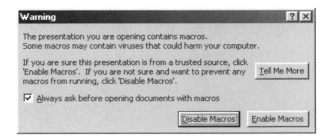

Figure 1.4 This warning is displayed when you Open certain presentations.

This is a warning telling you that the file you are opening contains macros (instructions to automate the presentation). We can ignore this message and simply click on the **Disable Macros** button to open the file.

The PowerPoint Central presentation should now be loaded and your screen should look as in Figure 1.5.

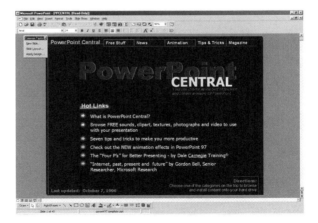

Figure 1.5 Slide one of the PowerPoint Central presentation file.

caution!

The previous instructions assume that when Microsoft Office was installed on your computer the standard default locations were used. If this is not the case then the file **Ppcentrl.pps** may be located somewhere else and you will have to use the Find options in the Open file dialogue box to locate it. If the file does not exist on your hard disk you can open it from the Office folder on the Microsoft Office CD-Rom.

Once **Ppcentrl.pps** has been opened in PowerPoint you can edit it to make any changes you wish.

4. For example, if you click on the text "**Last updated: October 7, 1996**" in the bottom left hand corner of the first slide and change the date to today's date, you can now save the new version of the presentation by following these steps:

5. On the Menu Bar click on **File | Save As...** and the **Save As** dialogue box will appear, as in Figure 1.6.

Figure 1.6 The Save As dialogue box with the file name highlighted.

6. Select the **My Documents** folder using the **Save in:** drop down list and type the filename '*Sample1*' in the **File name:** box, check that the **Save as type:** box says **Presentation** and click on the **Save** button.

information

Using the Save in: option you can specify any folder to save your presentations in. If you wish to save a presentation to a floppy diskette then select this option from the Save in: drop down list.

You can Open several different PowerPoint presentations at the same time by following steps 1 to 3 above and selecting the appropriate folders from which to load files. Similarly you can save any PowerPoint presentations by following steps 5 and 6 changing both the folder and filenames as appropriate.

7. To close a presentation click on the **File | Close** option on the **Menu Bar**.

If you have made any changes to an open presentation then when you try to close it you will be asked whether you wish to save the changes you have made to the file, for example:

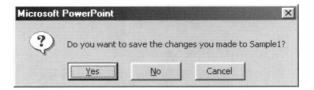

If you click on the Yes button then the file will be saved with the existing filename – overwriting the original version. However, if you wish to keep the original version of the file you should click on the No button and use the File | Save As... option from the Menu Bar to save the current open presentation with a different filename from the original.

Finally in this exercise we will look at the Help facilities available in PowerPoint which can provide you with online assistance when you need it. There are several different ways to trigger the help functions within PowerPoint and we will deal with each method in turn.

8. When you start PowerPoint you may have noticed a small window looking as in Figure 1.7.

Figure 1.7 The Office Assistant.

This is the Office Assistant and it is designed to provide you with help if you encounter problems when using the program. The Office Assistant like the normal Microsoft Help facilities is context sensitive which means that it tries to provide help based on what you are doing at the time.

information

There are several different "characters" available to act as Office Assistants and depending on how your version of Microsoft Office has been configured you may see any of the following characters, as in Figure 1.8.

Figure 1.8 The various Office Assistant "characters".

If you click on the Office Assistant then the following pop up dialogue box appears, as in Figure 1.9.

Figure 1.9 The Office Assistant asks you what you would like to do?

As you can see from the example in Figure 1.9 the Office Assistant already knows that you are at a point in the program where you are being prompted to either **Create a new presentation** or **Create my own template** and you can simply click on either of these options to get appropriate help. However, one of the best features of the Office Assistant is that you can simply type in a question and it will try to find the most appropriate help for you.

For example, type in the words "*Saving my work*" and click on the **Search** button. The Office Assistant should display a list of topics similar to that in Figure 1.10 for you to choose from.

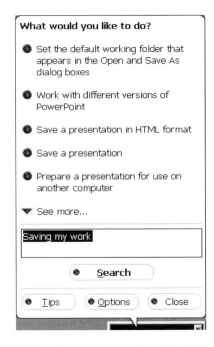

Figure 1.10 Performing a query using the Office Assistant.

Clicking on an item in the list will display the relevant Help topic.

9. As well as the Office Assistant you can access Help by clicking on the **Help** I **Contents** and **Index** option on the Menu Bar. This displays a window with 3 tabbed sections **Contents**, **Index** and **Find**.

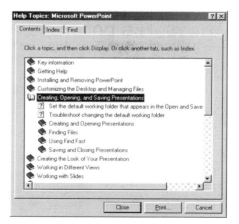

Figure 1.11 The Help Topics Contents tab showing sub sections.

The **Contents** tab presents you with a list of Help contents to select from. Note that the main sections may have sub-sections, as in Figure 1.11.

Figure 1.12 You can search for keywords in the Index section.

The **Index** tab displays a list of indexed keywords that are available in the help system. You simply click on the index word you want and then click on the Display button as in Figure 1.12.

**Figure 1.13 The Find sections lets
you look for any words or phrases.**

The **Find** tab allows you to search for any word or phrase and the Help
system will then show you any matches that it can find. Once again you can
simply click on any found topic and click on the Display button to see it as in
Figure 1.13.

**Help is always available in PowerPoint no matter what
actual task you are performing. The quickest way to get
help is to press the F1 on your keyboard.**

Whichever method you use to access the Help system in PowerPoint you will
be able to see step by step help on most topics as in Figure 1.14.

**Figure 1.14 A specific Help Topic on
how to Open a presentation.**

Summary

In this initial section on PowerPoint we have covered the procedures necessary to start the application and to open any existing presentation files. We have also looked at how to save presentations and how to use both the Office Assistant and the Help system to obtain help relevant to the procedures being carried out.

Fortunately, these basic tasks are common to all the modules in Microsoft Office, so once you have mastered these procedures in PowerPoint you should be able to cope with the same tasks in the other applications, such as Word or Excel.

1.2. Adjust Basic Settings

Now that we have looked at starting PowerPoint and opening and saving files we need to investigate the main PowerPoint screen in more detail.

In this section we will learn how to:

● Change display modes.
● Use the page view magnification tool/zoom tool.
● Modify the toolbar display.

Exercise 1.2

In this exercise we will look at how you can alter the way that PowerPoint displays information and how you can alter the appearance of PowerPoint itself.

If it is not already open you should start PowerPoint and open the **Sample1** presentation which we saved in the **My Documents** folder in Exercise 1.1. If you see the warning about macros simply click on the **Disable Macros** button. Your screen should look something like Figure 1.15.

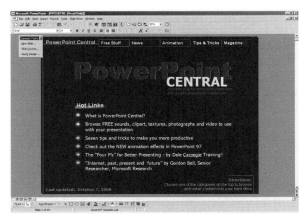

Figure 1.15 The PowerPoint screen after opening the Sample1 presentation.

If the **Office Assistant** window is displayed then close it by clicking on the top right hand corner. Similarly, you might have another small window displayed labelled **Common Tasks** which you can also close.

In PowerPoint you can change the way that a presentation is displayed on screen by using the view control buttons situated in the bottom left hand corner of the main window.

From left to right these buttons will allow you to select the following views:

1. Clicking on the **View Slide** button displays one slide at a time. Use this view to modify or edit a slide's contents. (Note that this is generally the default view when you open or create a presentation.)

2. Clicking on the **Outline View** button displays the entire presentation in the form of an outline listing the title and main topics for each slide as in Figure 1.16. Use this view to enter and edit text. (Note that this view is a useful way to see the structure of a presentation.)

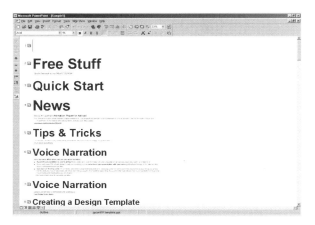

Figure 1.16 The Outline View.

step 3. Clicking on the **Slide Sorter View** button displays all the slides in a presentation in miniature as in Figure 1.17. Use this view to rearrange or add transition effects to your slides.

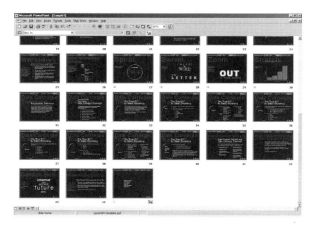

Figure 1.17 The Slide Sorter View.

step 4. Clicking on the **Notes Page View** button displays a reduced view of a slide with an area underneath for you to type in notes as in Figure 1.18. Use this view to add notes which can act as a prompt when you run a presentation.

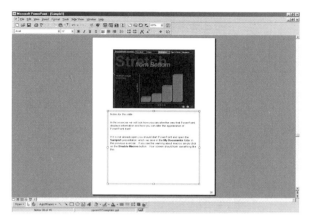

Figure 1.18 The Notes Page View.

5. Clicking on the **Slide Show View** button displays a presentation as a series of slides onscreen as in Figure 1.19. Use this view to check the appearance of your slides and to run through a presentation onscreen. (Note to exit from the Slide Show View press the Esc key on your keyboard.)

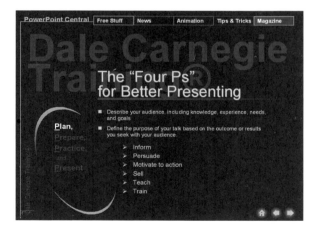

Figure 1.19 The Slide Show View.

When using the Slide Show View option you can view the slides full screen by clicking on the Browse I Fullscreen option on the Menu Bar.

You can change the magnification or zoom level in all of the views detailed above except the Slide Show View.

Controlling the magnification or zoom level can be achieved in two ways:

6. By using the **Zoom** icon control drop down list on the Standard Toolbar, as in Figure 1.20.

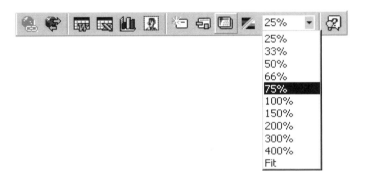

Figure 1.20 Using the Zoom icon to change magnification.

7. Or, by using the **View | Zoom...** option from the Menu Bar, which displays a window as in Figure 1.21.

Figure 1.21 The Zoom control window.

Finally in this exercise we shall look at how you modify the Toolbar display in PowerPoint.

PowerPoint has a total of 11 separate toolbars available and by default 3 of these are displayed as standard, two at the top of the screen and one at the bottom of the main screen:

Figure 1.22 The Standard Toolbar (top of screen by default).

Figure 1.23 The Formatting Toolbar (top of screen by default).

Figure 1.24 The Drawing Toolbar (bottom of screen by default).

8. You can control which of the 11 toolbars are visible by using the **View** | **Toolbars** option on the Menu Bar. Toolbars currently displayed are shown with a tick next to them as in Figure 1.25.

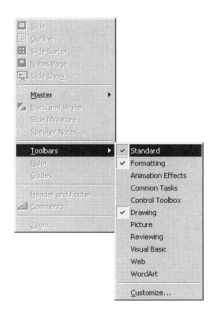

Figure 1.25 Selecting toolbars for displaying.

Summary

In this section we have looked at how you can view presentations in various modes in order to view individual slides, an outline of an entire presentation, miniature versions of slides for sorting and rearranging, add notes to slides, and to see a complete slide show. We have also looked at how you can use the Zoom controls to increase or decrease the size of an image being viewed. In addition, we looked at how to control the displaying of Toolbars.

You should now have a better understanding of the main elements of the PowerPoint screen and how to control and manage the display of information.

1.3. Document Exchange

PowerPoint uses its own file format with the file extension .ppt for storing presentations. However, there may be occasions when you need to save a presentation in a different format, for example to transfer text into a word processing package or to create an image from a slide.

In this section we will look at how you can:

● Save an existing presentation under another file format.
● Save a presentation in a format appropriate for posting to a Web Site.

Exercise 1.3

This exercise will look how you can save PowerPoint presentations or parts thereof in different formats.

If it is not already open you should start PowerPoint and open the **Sample1** presentation which we saved in the **My Documents** folder in Exercise 1.1. Once again if you see the warning about macros simply click on the **Disable Macros** button.

step **1.** When you click on the **File I Save As...** option on the Menu Bar the **Save As...** dialogue box appears, as in Figure 1.26.

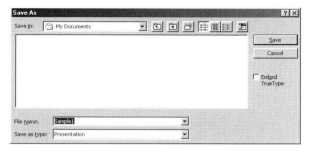

**Figure 1.26 The Save As... dialogue box where you
can decide on the target folder and file name.**

2. As well as being able to specify a filename and a location (folder) for saving
the presentation you can also specify the file type by clicking on the drop
down list on the **Save as type:** box as in Figure 1.27.

**Figure 1.27 Using the Save as type option to save
a presentation in a different file format.**

PowerPoint allows you to save a presentation in the following file formats:

Save as type	Extension	Use to save
Presentations	.ppt	A normal PowerPoint presentation.
Windows Metafile	.wmf	A slide as a graphic image.
Outline/RTF	.rtf	A presentation outline as a text file.
Presentation Templates	.pot	A presentation as a template for creating other similar presentations.
PowerPoint Show	.pps	A presentation that will always open as a slide show which cannot be edited.

For example, if you wish to save the text from a presentation so that it can be edited with a word processing package such as Microsoft Word then using the **Save as type:** drop down list select **Outline/RTF** and PowerPoint will create a file in the relevant format.

In addition, you can save a presentation in a format that is suitable for creating Web pages on the Internet. However, you cannot do this with the normal **File | Save As...** option on the Menu Bar and instead you have to use another menu option.

3. Clicking on the **File | Save as HTML...** option on the Menu Bar starts the **Save as HTML** Wizard which displays the dialogue box shown in Figure 1.28.

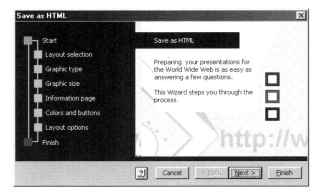

Figure 1.28 Using the Save as HTML wizard to save a presentation as a Web page.

From here all you need to do is follow the instructions to save your presentation in a format suitable for publishing Web pages on the Internet.

> **Wizard: A Wizard within Microsoft applications is a special feature which is designed to guide the user step by step through a complex process. There are many different types of Wizards included as standard with Microsoft Office and if you have access to the Internet you can download other Wizards that you might find useful from http://www.microsoft.com/downloads/search.asp?**

Summary

In this section we have covered the ways that you can save PowerPoint presentations in various formats so that the information that they contain can be used in other applications. We have also seen how it is possible to generate Web pages so that a presentation can be used on the Internet.

Review Questions

1. What is the basic procedure for starting PowerPoint from the Windows desktop?

2. Which keyboard key should you press to invoke the online Help in PowerPoint?

3. How many different display modes (or views) are available in PowerPoint?

4. Which view would you select to see a complete summary of a presentation?

5. Which 3 toolbars are displayed onscreen by default in PowerPoint?

6. Which Menu Bar option would you use to save a presentation in a format suitable for publishing as a Web page?

Basic Operations

In this chapter you will learn how to

- *Create a new presentation.*
- *Choose an appropriate automatic slide layout format for individual slides*
- *Modify a slide layout.*
- *Add text to a slide.*
- *Add an image from an image library.*
- *Use a master slide.*
- *Use the Copy and Paste tools to duplicate text, images or slides within the presentation or active presentations.*
- *Use the Copy and Paste tools to move text, images or slides within the presentation or active presentations.*
- *Delete selected text, images or slides.*
- *Re-order slides within the presentation.*

Now that you have a general feel about how PowerPoint works, we shall now expand on our knowledge by looking at some basic operations.

2.1. Create a Presentation

Up until now we have been using the Ppcentrl.ppt file and the Sample1.ppt for carrying out our exercises and whilst these have been useful in the early stages of understanding PowerPoint it is time we created our own presentation from scratch.

In this section we shall look at the following procedures:

● Create a new presentation.
● Choose an appropriate automatic slide layout format for individual slides.
● Modify slide layout.
● Add text.
● Add an image from an image library.
● Use a master slide.

Exercise 2.1

This exercise will involve creating a new presentation and looking at the options available for the automatic laying out of slides, modifying the slide layout, adding text and images to a slide, and the use of a master slide to control the overall format of a presentation.

For the purposes of this and subsequent exercises we will create a new presentation designed as a guide to 'Buying a House'. It doesn't matter whether you know anything about this subject as we are just using it as an example of the type of thing that presentation software like PowerPoint can be used for. We will keep things fairly simple to start with and you will be told what information should appear on each slide of the presentation.

If it is not already open you should start PowerPoint and make sure that there are no existing presentations open.

1. Click in the **File I New...** option on the Menu Bar and you should see the **New Presentation** dialogue box as shown in Figure 2.1.

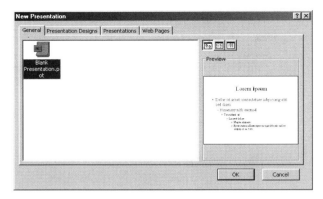

Figure 2.1 Creating a new presentation and choosing selecting a format.

2. The **General** tab should be showing and if it isn't then click on it. In the **General** tab section select the **Blank Presentation** icon and click on OK.

 information

> **PowerPoint comes with a wide range of templates (preformatted models for slides and presentations) which you can use to create your own presentations. These are useful in respect that they can save you a considerable amount of time designing fancy layouts and colour schemes.**

3. You should now see the **New Slide** dialogue box which allows you to choose the type or format of slide to create as in Figure 2.2.

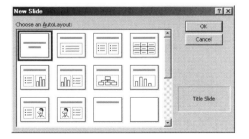

Figure 2.2 Choosing a slide format for a new slide.

ECDL

As you can see the New Slide dialogue box allows you to create several different types of slide with differing layouts. You can experiment with this option to see what effect each layout achieves.

4. Make sure the **AutoLayout** in the top left hand corner is selected and **Title Slide** is confirmed in the rectangle at the bottom right. Click on **OK** to accept your choice. Your screen should now look like Figure 2.3.

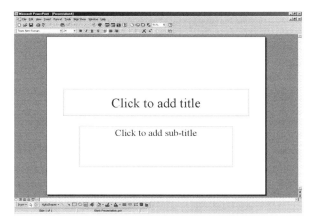

Figure 2.3 A new blank Title slide in Slide View.

On this slide you will see that there are two rectangles called 'Text Boxes' and we can use the mouse to drag the text box to a new position on the slide. To do this you need to position the mouse pointer on the text box boundary so that the cursor changes to the cross-shaped Move cursor and then click and drag the box to position it somewhere else. You can also re-size the text box by dragging on the box size control handles on the corners and edges.

5. Move the two text boxes and re-size them so that your slide looks like Figure 2.4.

Figure 2.4 The text boxes after they have been resized and moved.

6. Now we need to add some text to our first slide so click on the words **Click to add title** and type in '*Buying A House*', then click anywhere outside the text box. Similarly, in the lower text box type in the text '*A simple guide for first time purchasers*'. Your slide should now look like Figure 2.5.

Figure 2.5 The Title slide after adding text.

Our first slide is the title of the presentation and next we need to create some additional slides for the rest of the presentation.

7. Click on the **Insert I New Slide...** option on the Menu Bar and in the **New Slide** dialogue box you should see the second **AutoLayout** highlighted –

this is a **Bulleted List** layout (if it isn't selected click on it once to select it) then click on OK. Your new slide should look like Figure 2.6.

Figure 2.6 A new Bulleted List slide.

8. Now add text to each of the text boxes so that your slide looks like Figure 2.7.

Figure 2.7 The Bulleted List slide with text added.

When adding text to a Bulleted List, each time you press the return or enter key a new bullet appears automatically. Press the backspace key to delete any unwanted bullet points. If you press the Tab key then a new bullet level is created so that you can have indented bulleted text, like this:

● **Heading**
- **Subheading1**
- **Subheading2**
- **Subheading3**
- **Etc.**

To return to the previous level of indented bullets hold down the Shift and press the Tab key on your keyboard.

9. Now using the procedure in steps 8 and 9 above create the following additional slides which will appear as slides 3 to 7 in your presentation as in Figure 2.8.

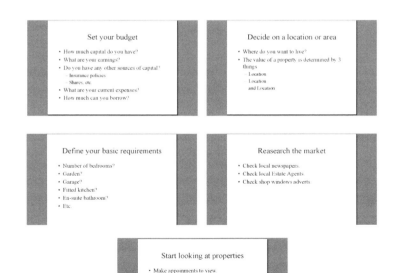

Figure 2.8 Your additional slides.

You should now have a total of seven slides in your presentation with the first slide being a Title Slide and the remaining six being Bulleted List slides.

10. Before we go any further we should save the work we have done on our presentation so far. So, click on the **File | Save** option on the Menu Bar and save the presentation with the filename '*House*' in the folder **My Documents**.

11. As well as text, PowerPoint slides can contain pictures or graphics images. We shall now put a picture on slide number 4 of our House presentation. Make sure that slide 4 is displayed in PowerPoint by clicking on the **Slide Sorter View** and then double clicking on slide number 4.

12. To insert a picture in a slide select **Insert | Picture | Clip Art...** on the Menu Bar. This opens up the Clip Gallery where you can select a category by clicking on it as in Figure 2.9.

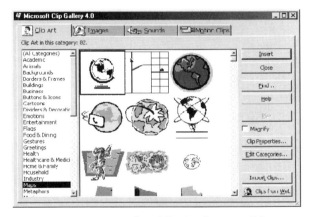

Figure 2.9 Inserting Clip Art into a slide.

13. Select a likely category such as **Maps** and choose an image.

14. Once you have found a suitable image, click on the Insert button so that the selected image will be inserted into your slide.

caution!

Depending on which version of the Microsoft Gallery has been installed on your PC you might see a windows which is slightly different than that shown in Figure 2.9. This applies to Gallery version 4.

If your system is using Gallery version 5 you will see a dialogue box as shown in Figure 2.10 and when you select a category you will see a new dialogue as in Figure 2.11 from where you can select a specific image.

Figure 2.10 Category display in Gallery version 5.

Figure 2.11 Clip art image display in Gallery version 5.

When you select a Clip Art image in Gallery version 5 a pop up menu appears as in Figure 2.12 so that you can insert the image into your slide.

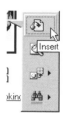

Figure 2.12 The insert image pop up menu in Gallery version 5.

Whichever version of the Microsoft Gallery you are using the new image will appear in the centre of the target slide, as shown in Figure 2.13.

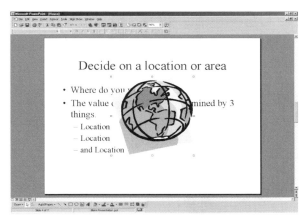

Figure 2.13 Newly inserted Clip Art images appear in the centre of a slide.

15. Now you can use the box size control handles and the mouse pointer to resize and move the image to an appropriate position on the slide. For example, as shown in Figure 2.14.

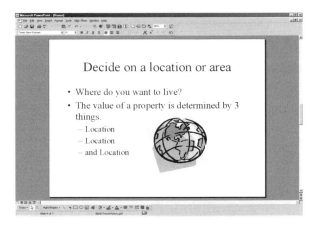

Figure 2.14 Our new graphic image after it has been resized and repositioned.

16. Once again save your presentation using the **File I Save** option on the Menu Bar before proceeding to the next part of this exercise.

Occasionally you might wish to have exactly the same information on every slide within a presentation (for example a company name or logo) and whilst you could do this manually PowerPoint has a much more convenient method of achieving this called the Slide Master.

step **17.** To view the Slide Master select **View | Master | Slide Master** from the Menu Bar and your display should change to the layout shown in Figure 2.15.

Figure 2.15 The Slide Master ready to be edited.

step **18.** Click on the box marked **Footer Area** and type '*ABC Presentation Services*' then click on the **Close** button in the small window labelled **Master** on the screen. You will now be returned to your presentation and every slide will have the words 'ABC Presentation Service' on the bottom, as in Figure 2.16.

- Location
- and Location!

ABC Presentation Services

Figure 2.16 The new footer details shown on every slide.

step **19.** Finally, save your presentation using the **File | Save** option on the Menu Bar.

caution!

You cannot edit the Footer text on the individual slides in your presentation as it was created using the Slide Master. You must re-edit the Slide Master itself to change the Footer and any changes will then be reflected in all normal presentation slides.

★ ECDL ★

Summary

In this section we have covered the creation of a very simple presentation and seen how to add both text and images to a slide. We have also seen how making changes to the Slide Master can alter the appearance of every slide in a presentation.

2.2. Copy, Move, Delete-Text

Editing slides in a presentation is one of the most fundamental aspects of using PowerPoint and in this section we will cover the following procedures:

- Use the Copy and Paste tools to duplicate text within the presentation or active presentations.
- Use the Cut and Paste tools to move text within the presentation or active presentations.
- Delete selected text.

Exercise 2.2

1. If it is not already open then open our presentation House.ppt and make sure that you are positioned on slide one.

2. Double click on the word **House** in the top text box to select it, as in Figure 2.17.

Buying A House

Figure 2.17 A portion of text selected is shown as white on black.

3. Select **Edit I Copy** on the Menu Bar to copy the selected text into the Clipboard.

4. Next click just to the left of the word **purchasers** in the lower text box to establish an insertion point as shown in Figure 2.18.

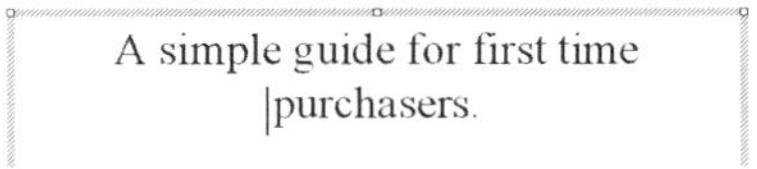

A simple guide for first time
|purchasers.

Figure 2.18 Marking the insertion point.

5. Now if you select **Edit | Paste** from the Menu Bar the text which was copied to the Clipboard will be inserted just before the word **purchasers**, as in Figure 2.19.

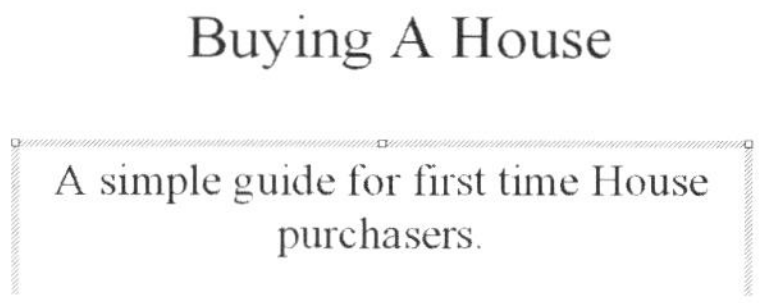

Buying A House

A simple guide for first time House
purchasers.

Figure 2.19 Slide after insertion of the word House.

Instead of using the Menu Bar to perform Copy, Cut and Paste functions via the Clipboard you can click on the appropriate icons on the Standard Toolbar.

Notice that the original selected text "House" remains where it was in the topmost text box. If we want to Move the word "House" we can select it and use the option Edit | Cut to remove it from its original position and then Edit | Paste to insert it wherever it is required. We can also simply Delete the word "House" by either selecting it and pressing the Delete key on the keyboard or omitting the Paste function after performing an Edit | Cut operation.

Using the Copy, Cut and Paste functions along with the clipboard allows you to not only move, copy and delete selected items within an individual presentation, but also enables you to move and copy them between any active (Open) presentations as well. Simply select an item and either copy or cut it to the clipboard and then switch to another open presentation before performing the paste operation and the item will be either moved or copied between presentations.

6. Now select the word **House** which appears between **time** and **purchasers** and delete it using either the Delete key on the keyboard or by using **Edit | Cut** or by clicking on the **Cut** icon. Finally, save your presentation using the **File | Save** option on the Menu Bar.

caution!

> **The Windows Clipboard only stores one item at a time. Whenever you use the Edit I Paste function whatever was last cut or copied to the Clipboard is pasted and this might not always be what you intended. Therefore you should consider Cut and Paste or Copy and Paste as a single function.**

Summary

In this section we have seen how we can use the Windows Clipboard combined with PowerPoint's Cut, Copy, and Paste functions to copy, move, or delete text on the slides within our presentation.

2.3. Copy, Move, Delete-Images

Just as we can copy, move, and delete text on slides in PowerPoint we can perform the same operations on images. In this section we see how we can:

- Use the Copy and Paste tools to duplicate an image within the presentation or active presentations.
- Use the Cut and Paste tools to move an image within the presentation or active presentations.
- Delete an image.

Exercise 2.3

1. Once again, if it is not already open then open our presentation House.ppt and make sure that you are positioned on slide 4.

2. Select the picture on this slide by clicking on it once, as shown in Figure 2.20.

of a property is determined by 3

tion

Figure 2.20 Selecting an image on a slide.

step **3.** We can now use the same Cut, Copy, and Paste functions as described in the previous exercise to move, copy or delete the selected image.

step **4.** Make a copy of the image and paste it onto slide number 5, resizing it if necessary, so that slide 5 now looks like Figure 2.21.

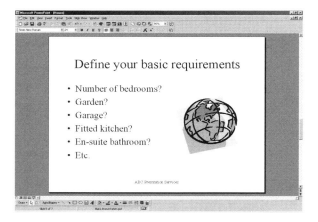

Figure 2.21 Slide number 5 with the copied image inserted.

step **5.** Finally, save your presentation using the **File I Save** option on the Menu Bar.

Summary

In this section we have seen how to use the Windows Clipboard combined with PowerPoint's Cut, Copy, and Paste functions to copy, move, or delete images on the slides within our presentation.

2.4. Copy, Move, Delete-Slides

Finally, on the subject of Basic Operations we will:

● Use the Copy and Paste tools to duplicate a slide within the presentation or active presentations.
● Use the Cut and Paste tools to move a slide within the presentation or active presentations.
● Re-order slides within the presentation.
● Delete a slide/slides within the presentation.

Exercise 2.4

step **1.** Once again, if it is not already open then open our presentation House.ppt. (It doesn't matter which slide is displayed.)

step **2.** Click on the **Slide Sorter View** to display all 7 slides in our presentation, as in Figure 2.22.

Figure 2.22 The Slide Sorter View showing 7 slides in miniature.

step **3.** We can now use the same Cut, Copy and Paste functions as described in the previous exercise to move or copy any selected slides. To delete a slide from a presentation in the Slide Sorter View, simply select it and press the Delete key on the keyboard or choose Edit | Delete Slide from the menu bar. If you want to delete multiple slides then holding down the Ctrl key will allow you to select more than one slide at a time.

step **4.** Move and copy a few slides and when you have finished, close our presentation without saving it so that the original order is preserved.

shortcut

If you want to simply move a slide to a different position in the Slide Sorter View in order to change the order of the slides you can just drag and drop them using the mouse. This saves having to cut and paste them using the clipboard.

Summary

In this section we have seen how to use the Windows Clipboard combined with PowerPoint's Cut, Copy, and Paste functions to copy, move, or delete slides within the Slide Sorter View.

Review Questions

1. What is a template and why would you want to use one?

2. What type of object is used to hold text on a slide?

3. How can you indent a Bulleted List to produce sub sections?

4. Which Menu Bar options would you use to open up the Clip Gallery in order to select an image to appear on a slide?

5. What is the principle use of the Slide Master in PowerPoint presentations?

6. How many items can be stored in the Windows Clipboard at any one time?

7. Which display view would you use if you wanted to rearrange the order of slides in a presentation?

8. What procedure would you use to make an exact copy of a slide to be placed somewhere else in a presentation?

Formatting

In this chapter you will learn how to

- *Change the font type of text.*
- *Centre and align text.*
- *Apply italics, bold, underlining and case changes to text.*
- *Apply shadow to text.*
- *Apply different colours to text font.*
- *Adjust line spacing.*
- *Change the type of bullets in a list.*
- *Re-size and move a text box within a slide.*
- *Set the line weights, style and colours of a text box.*

One of the main features of PowerPoint is the ability to change the appearance of text and text boxes on a slide. By using different fonts, styles, colours and other attributes you can enhance the look of slides and make them appear much more attractive and interesting. You can change the format of text in a text box by using either the Formatting Toolbar or by using the options under the Format command on the Menu Bar. However, the actual text boxes themselves can only be altered by using the Format command on the Menu Bar.

definition

Text Attributes: Text consists of a font, point size, and a style e.g. Arial font, 16 point, bold, italic, underline. Each of these settings is called an attribute and you can use them to alter the way that text appears both on the screen and when it is printed out.

In this section you will learn how to do the following:

● Format Text.
● Modify Text Boxes.

3.1. Format Text

Text on a slide is always contained within a place holder called a text box or an Autoshape. When you create a new slide a number of Autoshapes will be generated automatically depending on which Autolayout you choose. You can add a text box to a slide by using the **Insert | Text Box** menu option and then simply drawing the boundaries using the mouse.

Existing text can be formatted in a several ways and you can for example:

● Change the font type.
● Centre text, align text: left and right, top and bottom.
● Apply italics, bold, underlining and case changes to text.
● Apply shadow to text, use subscript and superscript.
● Apply different colours to the text font.
● Adjust line spacing.
● Change the type of bullets in a list.

Exercise 3.1

For this exercise we will format the basic slideshow which we created earlier so that it looks more interesting.

1. Open the presentation House.ppt and make sure that you are positioned on slide one.

2. Click once on the text at the top and the Autoshape box will be highlighted, as in Figure 3.1.

Figure 3.1 An Autoshape that has been selected.

3. Select the text with the mouse and then select **Format I Font...** from the menu options. The **Font** dialogue box will be displayed, as in Figure 3.2.

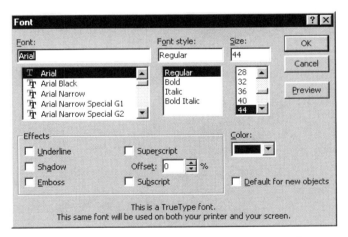

Figure 3.2 The Font dialogue box allows you to change text attributes.

4. Select **Arial** from the **Font:** list and click on **OK**. The text will now be displayed in Arial font, as in Figure 3.3.

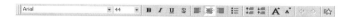

Buying a House

Figure 3.3 The text shown in Arial font.

The **Formatting Toolbar** can be used to quickly change text attributes. Simply select the target text and click on the appropriate icons on the Toolbar. For example, click on the **Bold** icon to change text to bold, click on the **Italic** icon to change text to italic, click on the **Underline** icon to underline text, and click on the **Shadow** icon to produce shadowed text.

When we first entered this text it was automatically centred with the Autoshape frame but we can if we wish change the alignment using the **Format I Alignment** menu options or by using the **Formatting** Toolbar.

Horizontal text alignment is easy but if we want to align text vertically within an Autoshape or a text box we need to use a slightly different technique.

5. Click on the text underneath the main heading and then select the **Format I Autoshape...** menu option. A dialogue box appears with 5 tabbed sections. Select the **Text Box** tab as in Figure 3.4.

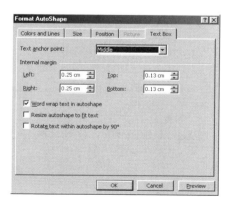

Figure 3.4 Aligning text in the middle of a text box.

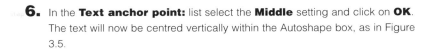

6. In the **Text anchor point:** list select the **Middle** setting and click on **OK**. The text will now be centred vertically within the Autoshape box, as in Figure 3.5.

A simple guide for first time purchasers.

Figure 3.5 Text aligned in the middle of a text box.

When you make any adjustments using the Format Autoshape dialogue box you can check the effect by simply clicking on the Preview button. This allows you to easily change your mind before clicking on the OK button to accept the changes.

7. Text attributes or styles such as bold, italic or underline can be easily applied to selected text using either the **Formatting** Toolbar or via **Format I Font...** from the menu options. However, PowerPoint has another neat feature that allows you to quickly change the case of any selected text.

8. Select the heading text on our slide and then select **Format I Change Case...** and a small dialogue box will appear, as in Figure 3.6.

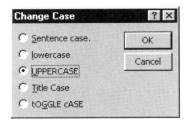

Figure 3.6 The Change Case option box.

9. Select the **UPPERCASE** option and click on **OK**. The heading will now be in all capital letters.

Other text attributes that can be applied to text include Shadow, Subscript and Superscript. Shadow can be applied by clicking on the **Shadow** button on the **Formatting** Toolbar but you need to use the **Format I Font...** menu option to apply or remove Subscript or Superscript on selected text.

Subscript and Superscript: Subscript positions text slightly below the line whilst Superscript positions text slightly above the line. For example, this is SUBSCRIPT and this is SUPERSCRIPT.

10. Once again select the heading text and click on the **Shadow** button on the **Formatting** Toolbar. Your heading should now look like Figure 3.7.

Figure 3.7 Shadow effect on text.

The use of colour is one of the most effective ways of emphasising text and PowerPoint allows you to change the colour of any selected text.

11. Select our heading text again and then select **Format I Font...** from the menu options.

12. From the **Color:** list select **More Colors:** and the dialogue box shown in Figure 3.8 will appear.

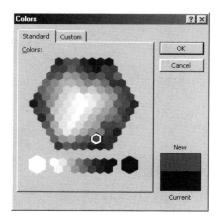

Figure 3.8 Selecting different colours for fonts.

13. You can now simply click on a colour and then click on **OK** and the text will change accordingly.

If you can't see the colour that you want on the Standard tab in the Colors dialogue box then you can mix your own using the Custom tab.

As well as changing the colour of text you can adjust the spacing between lines of text on a slide.

14. Click on the text underneath the main heading and then select the **Format** I **Line Spacing...** menu option. The **Line Spacing** dialogue box shown in Figure 3.9 will appear:

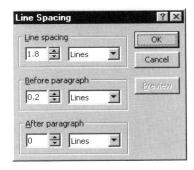

Figure 3.9 Changing the spacing between lines of text.

15. Here you can adjust the various line spacing settings by typing in new values (in number of lines or font point sizes) or by using the up/down arrow ('spinner') control to increase or decrease the values. The **Preview** button lets you see the changes before applying them with the **OK** button.

Finally, we can change the types of bullets used in a bulleted list of text items.

16. Select slide 2 in our House Buying presentation. (Remember that when we created this slide we specified Bulleted List as the Autolayout choice.)

17. Select the text in the bulleted list and then select **Format** I **Bullet...** from the menu options. The **Bullet** dialogue box will appear as shown in Figure 3.10. This allows us to select any character to use as a bullet and you can also specify its colour and size.

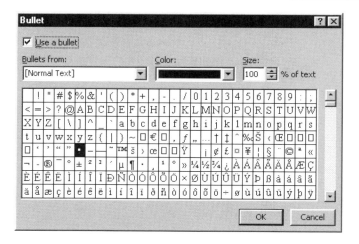

Figure 3.10 Choosing an alternative bullet character.

step **18.** Choose a character and then click on **OK**.

caution!

Whilst you can select a number rather than a character to use as a bullet, the same number will be used for ALL the items in the bulleted list. This is not the same as a numbered list in which the items are numbered sequentially. The bulleting options within PowerPoint do not cater for a numbered list and you will have to number items manually.

step **19.** Close the presentation saving any changes made.

3.2. Modify Text Boxes

As well as formatting text on a slide we can also format the actual text boxes. We can for example:

● Re-size and move a text box within a slide.
● Set line weights, style and colours of a text box.

Exercise 3.2

step **1.** If it is not already open then open our presentation House.ppt and make sure that you are positioned on slide one.

2. Click on the heading text and then using the mouse drag the text box to a new position on the slide. To do this you need to position the mouse pointer on the text box boundary so that the cursor changes to the Move cursor and then click and drag.

You can re-size the text box by dragging on the box size control handles.

3. To alter the line weights, style and colours of a text box click on the heading text and then select **Format | Autoshape...** on the menu options.

4. Select the **Colors and Lines** tab as shown in Figure 3.11.

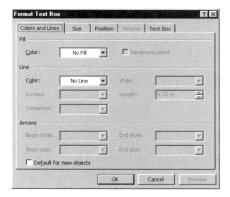

Figure 3.11 Changing the colour of lines round Autoshapes.

Here we can select different Fill (background) Colours, Line Colours, Line Styles (e.g. double), Dashed Lines, and Line Weights (thickness). Experiment with these settings using the **Preview** button to check the results. Once you are happy click on the **OK** button.

Figure 3.12 shows an example of the sort of effects you can achieve:

BUYING A HOUSE

Figure 3.12 A text box with a patterned border and graduated fill background.

5. Close the presentation saving any changes made.

Summary

In this section we have covered the various ways that both text and text boxes can be formatted in order to enhance their appearance. This ability to apply formatting to such elements is one of the key features of PowerPoint and it allows you to be fairly creative in the design of your presentation slides.

The vast range of options and choices available can be a bit bewildering at first but if you are prepared to experiment then you can produce some very interesting looking results.

Review Questions

1. What are text attributes?

2. Which Menu Bar option would you use to centre the text inside a text box or an Autoshape?

3. What is the difference between subscript and superscript?

4. When setting Line Spacing what two separate units of measurement are available?

5. What are control handles and what are they used for?

6. Which Menu Bar option would you use to change the background colour of a text box or Autoshape?

Graphics and Charts

In this chapter you will learn how to

- *Add different types of lines to a slide.*
- *Change the line colour and modify the width.*
- *Add various forms of shapes such as boxes and circles to a slide.*
- *Add a free drawn line to a slide.*
- *Change the attributes of a shape by colouring it in or changing the line type.*
- *Apply shadow to a shape.*
- *Rotate or flip a drawn object in a slide.*
- *Create and modify an organisational chart.*
- *Create different kinds of charts such as bar charts and pie charts.*
- *Import images from other files.*
- *Re-size and move an image in a slide.*
- *Import objects such as text, spreadsheets or graphic files to slide.*
- *Copy an imported object to a master slide.*
- *Add border effects to an object.*

You may have already noticed the **Drawing** Toolbar which by default appears at the bottom of the main PowerPoint window. If it isn't displayed on your screen just use option **View** I **Toolbars** I **Drawing** on the Menu Bar to display it. Using the drawing capabilities of PowerPoint you can embellish and enhance your presentation slides by adding graphical objects such as lines, boxes, circles, and other shapes.

In addition, you can include other graphical elements like charts and graphs. These graphical elements can be created within PowerPoint or they can be created in another application, such as, a spreadsheet and then imported into your presentation.

4.1. Drawn Objects

We shall start off by looking at Drawn Objects and how we can:

- Add different types of lines to a slide.
- Move lines in a slide.
- Change line colour/modify line width.
- Add various forms of shape; boxes, circles etc. to a slide. Add a free drawn line.
- Change the attributes of the shape; colour in the shape, change the line type.
- Apply shadow to a shape.
- Rotate or flip a drawn object in a slide.

Exercise 4.1

For this exercise we will continue to enhance our existing presentation.

step **1.** Open the presentation House.ppt and make sure that you are positioned on slide one which should look similar to Figure 4.1.

Figure 4.1 Slide one of House.ppt.

2. On the **Draw** Toolbar click on the **Line** icon and using the mouse draw a line anywhere on the slide.

If you want vertical or horizontal lines hold down the Shift key on the keyboard whilst you are drawing them with the mouse.

3. If you select a line that you have drawn you can move it to a new position when the cursor changes to a cross by simply clicking and dragging.

4. When a drawn line is selected you will notice that it has control handles at either end which can be used to either resize the line or to change its orientation.

5. Also whilst the line is selected you can alter its appearance by selecting **Format I Colors and Lines...** on the Menu Bar, as shown in Figure 4.2. Here we can select different Line Colours, Line Styles (e.g. double), Dashed Lines, Line Weights (thickness), and Arrows (on either end of the line or both ends), as in Figure 4.3. Experiment with these settings using the **Preview** button to check the results. Once you are happy with any of your changes click on the **OK** button.

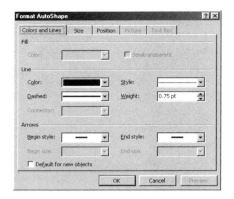

Figure 4.2 Altering the attributes of a line.

Figure 4.3 Examples of lines formats.

6. As well as drawing lines on your slides you can use the **Drawing** Toolbar to draw a variety of other simple objects, such as rectangles and ovals, as shown in Figure 4.4. For example, to draw a box on a slide click on the **Rectangle** icon and then click anywhere on the slide to place the object; you can then move or resize the object as required.

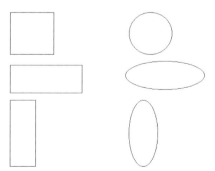

Figure 4.4 Examples of simple rectangles and ovals.

To draw perfect squares or circles hold down the Shift key on the keyboard whilst resizing a rectangle or oval.

7. More sophisticated objects called 'Autoshapes' can also be drawn by selecting the **Autoshapes** button on the **Drawing** Toolbar and then choosing a shape from any of the categories provided in the drop down list, as shown in Figure 4.5.

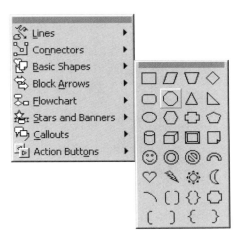

Figure 4.5 Selecting different types of Autoshape.

8. It is even possible to create a freehand drawn shape using the **AutoShapes I Lines I Freeform** option. So you could create objects like the example shown in Figure 4.6.

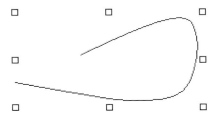

Figure 4.6 A Freeform drawn line.

9. Once you have drawn an object on a slide you can use the **Format I Autoshape...** option on the Menu Bar to change its appearance. With a bit of practice it is possible to create almost any desired drawn object using the tools provided. Figure 4.7 shows an example of what can be achieved using the PowerPoint drawing tools.

Figure 4.7 An example of a drawing.

step 10. In order to enhance simple drawn objects you can use the **Shadow** icon on the **Drawing** Toolbar to add special shadow effects. There are several effects to choose from as shown in Figure 4.8 and you should experiment with these to see how they can change the look of an object.

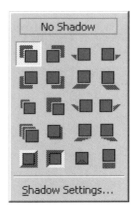

Figure 4.8 Different shadow effects are available.

step 11. Finally, on the subject of drawn objects you can rotate an object using either the **Size** tab on the **Format Autoshape** option and adjusting the **Rotation:** angle, as shown in Figure 4.9 or by clicking in the **Free Rotate** icon on the **Drawing** Toolbar as in Figure 4.10.

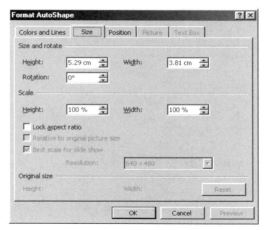

Figure 4.9 Using the Format Autoshape option to rotate an object.

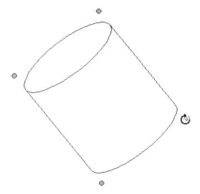

Figure 4.10 Using the Free Rotate tool to rotate an object.

Summary

In this section we have covered the various procedures for creating drawn objects on slides and the options available for enhancing their appearance. As you can probably now appreciate PowerPoint has some very powerful and flexible drawing tools which allow you to be very creative.

Once again the vast range of options and choices available can be a bit bewildering at first but with a little practice you can create some excellent drawn objects to enhance your presentations.

4.2. Charts

One of the most common uses of applications such as PowerPoint is to present information in a graph or chart format. Therefore we shall now look at how we can:

● Create an organisational chart.
● Modify the structure of an organisational chart.
● Create different kinds of charts such as a bar chart, pie chart etc.

Exercise 4.2

For this exercise we will create a new presentation called 'Charts'.

If it is not already open you should start PowerPoint and make sure that there are no existing presentations open.

1. Click in the **File I New...** option on the Menu Bar and you should see the **New Presentation** dialogue box, as in Figure 4.11.

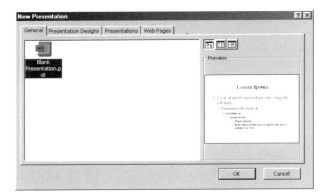

Figure 4.11 Creating a new presentation.

2. The **General** tab should be showing and if it isn't then click on it. In the **General** tab section select the **Blank Presentation** icon and click on **OK**.

3. You should now see the **New Slide** dialogue box shown in Figure 4.12 which allows you to choose the type or format of slide to create. For this exercise you should select the **Blank** slide format.

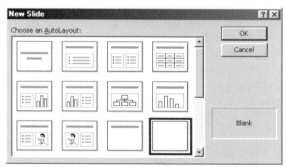

Figure 4.12 Creating a new "blank" slide.

4. On the Menu Bar select **Insert I Picture I Organization Chart** and a new window similar to Figure 4.13 should appear.

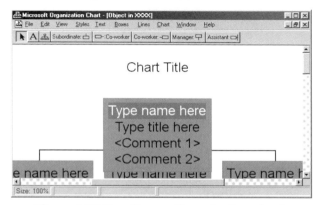

Figure 4.13 Creating an Organisation chart.

5. Here you can enter the details about people within an organisation by overtyping the prompts provided. A toolbar as shown in Figure 4.14 is provided so that you can easily add new boxes to your organisation and there are numerous formatting options available to enhance the appearance of the organisation chart. For example, to add a Subordinate, click on the ⎡Subordinate: ⎤ icon on the Toolbar and then click on the box of the person to whom to subordinate will report and a new box will appear underneath the selected superior for you to enter the subordinate details. Similarly, you can add a co-worker to either the left or right of another person by clicking on the appropriate ⎡□⊢:Co-worker⎤ or ⎡Co-worker: ⊣□⎤ icons.

Figure 4.14 The Organisation Chart toolbar.

6. Once you have finished entering the details and formatting your organisation chart you should click on **File I Close** and **Return to XXXX** (where **XXXX** is the name of your current presentation). When you do this you may be asked whether you wish to **Update Object in XXXX** as shown in Figure 4.15 before proceeding in which case you should click on the **Yes** button.

Figure 4.15 Confirmation of whether to update the Organisation Chart in XXXX.

7. You should now be returned to PowerPoint with your new organisation chart placed in the centre of your current slide. It may look something like that shown in Figure 4.16.

Figure 4.16 An example of an Organisation Chart.

8. If you wish to modify the structure of an organisation chart then double click on the chart in PowerPoint and the **Microsoft Organization Chart** windows will re-open. You can click and drag any of the boxes to new positions and the structure of the organisation will alter accordingly. In this way it is very easy to promote or demote staff within the organisation. It is best to experiment with this option in order to understand how it works.

Charts within PowerPoint are discrete objects and whilst you can resize and move them you cannot edit the contents unless you start the underlying application which was used to create them by double clicking on the chart.

9. As well as organisation charts there are other types of charts or graphs which can be created in PowerPoint. In our current presentation insert a new blank slide. Now select **Insert I Chart...** from the Menu Bar and a new chart object will appear on our slide, as in Figure 4.17.

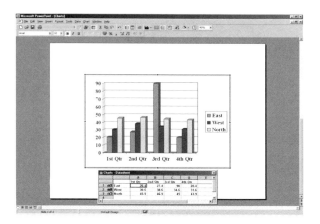

Figure 4.17 Creating a new chart.

10. By default a simple Column Chart is generated and just below it there is a small spreadsheet-like window labelled **Charts – Datasheet** containing some sample data, as in Figure 4.18. This is the source data for the chart displayed above it and whatever information you put in this spreadsheet will be reflected in the chart itself. Try changing one or two of the values in the columns A, B, C, and D to see what happens. When you have finished editing your chart data you can close the **Charts – Datasheet** window and the actual chart will remain on the slide. To re-open the **Charts – Datasheet** windows click on **View I Datasheet** on the Menu Bar.

		A	B	C	D	E
		1st Qtr	2nd Qtr	3rd Qtr	4th Qtr	
1	East	20.4	27.4	90	20.4	
2	West	30.6	38.6	34.6	31.6	
3	North	45.9	46.9	45	43.9	
4						

Presentation2 - Datasheet

Figure 4.18 The Charts – Datasheet with sample data in it.

11. Whilst the default chart type is a simple Column Chart you can create different styles of chart by clicking on **Chart I Chart Type...** and a tabbed **Chart Type** window appears, as shown in Figure 4.19.

caution!

Certain types of Charts are designed to only plot a single Data Series, for example Pie Charts. This means that if you change the Chart Type then not all the selected data may be plotted. For instance, in our example above the data for the chart shown in Figure 4.18 has 3 separate series for each of the regions and if you convert the Column chart to a Pie chart then only one of these regions will be plotted. Therefore you must take care when you are converting between different types of chart as sometimes the results might not be what you expected.

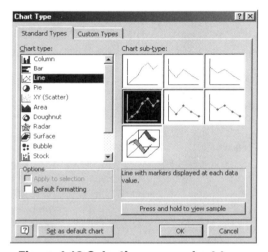

Figure 4.19 Selecting a new chart type.

Summary

In this section we have seen how to create and modify organisation charts in PowerPoint and looked at the various other types of charts that you can create on your presentation slides. We have seen how PowerPoint treats charts as special objects and by double clicking on a chart you can alter its appearance.

Creating and editing charts is a completely separate application in PowerPoint and there are hundreds of different options and settings for you to use in order to achieve the desired results.

4.3. Images & Other Objects

As we have seen it is fairly easy to create charts within PowerPoint but what happens if we want to use information from another application in our presentation? Well, fortunately it is possible to 'import' information from various applications and in this section we will see how to:

● Import images from other files.
● Re-size and move an image in a slide.
● Import other objects: text, spreadsheet, table, chart or graphic files to a slide.
● Copy an imported object to a master slide.
● Add border effects to an object.

Exercise 4.3

For this exercise we will continue to use our presentation called 'Charts'.

1. Start by inserting a new blank slide.

2. Click on **Insert I Object...** on the Menu Bar and the window shown in Figure 4.20 should appear.

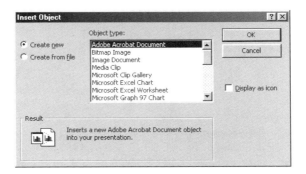

Figure 4.20 Inserting an object into a slide.

3. Select the **Create from file** option and the window should change to look like Figure 4.21.

Figure 4.21 Inserting an object from a file.

4. Here you can either type the name of the file you want to insert or use the **Browse...** button to look for a particular file. So, click on **Browse** and find a suitable image file to insert.

5. Once inserted the object can be resized or moved anywhere on the slide using the mouse, as in the example shown in Figure 4.22 showing the sound clip icon being moved to a new position on the slide. If you double click on the object you will start the application that was used to create it.

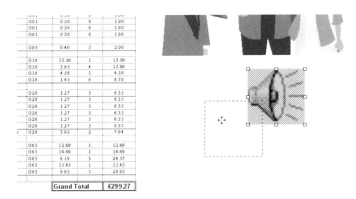

Figure 4.22 Moving an object on a slide by dragging with the mouse.

6. Practically any file can be inserted into a PowerPoint slide as an object. For example, you might wish to include data from a spreadsheet in a presentation and the easiest way to do this is to select **Insert I Object...** and choose the option to **Create from file**. You will then be able to browse for a particular spreadsheet file and insert its contents directly on to a slide without having to retype all the data. It is also possible to include audio or video clips on a slide which will play automatically when you double click on them with the mouse.

7. Any objects can be inserted on to the Slide Master provided that you switch to Slide Master view by selecting **View I Master I Slide Master** from the menu bar first. You can also copy and paste objects from other slides to the Slide Master via the clipboard. Objects inserted on the Slide Master will automatically appear on ALL slides in the presentation.

8. Finally, you can add border effects to an object by using the **Patterned Lines...** option on the **Format Object I Colors and Lines** tab, as shown in Figure 4.23.

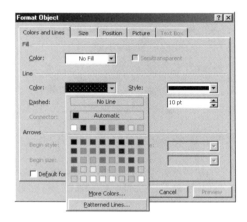

Figure 4.23 Formatting an object's border.

9. Here you can select different patterns for the lines around objects, as in Figure 4.24.

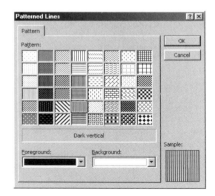

Figure 4.24 Choosing a pattern for the object border line.

step **10.** Note that in order for patterned lines to be effective you will generally need to increase the Line Weight (thickness) so that the pattern can be seen, as in the examples shown in Figure 4.25.

Figure 4.25 Examples of patterned borders around objects.

Summary

In this section we have seen how different types of objects can be placed on slides and how double clicking on an object can start the application that created it. Using objects is a great way to enhance a presentation but it can be quite difficult to achieve the correct effects so you might need to experiment a little first.

Review Questions

1. When drawing lines on a slide how can you ensure that they are perfectly vertical or horizontal?

2. How would you increase or decrease the length of a line which has been drawn on a slide?

3. If you wanted to sketch something on a slide which Autoshape options would you use?

4. There are two ways you can rotate an object on a slide. Can you describe both methods?

5. What Menu Bar option would you use to create an organisation chart on a slide?

6. Why can't you edit a chart directly within PowerPoint?

7. What happens when you double click on an object that has been inserted from another file?

8. Why might you need to increase the thickness of borders around objects?

Printing and Distribution

In this chapter you will learn how to

- *Select the appropriate output format for a slide presentation.*

- *Change the orientation of a slide to either landscape or portrait.*

- *Add notes to slides to assist the presenter.*

- *Number slides.*

- *Spell-check the text content of slides and amend where necessary.*

- *Preview a presentation document in slide, outline, slide sorter, or notes view.*

- *Print slides in various views and output formats.*

Now that we have created some presentations we need to think about printing and distribution of the material. Whilst many presentations will be given as slide shows on the computer itself, PowerPoint has some useful features which can help you prepare presentation materials in different formats for different purposes, such as outlines, handouts and speaker notes.

5.1. Slide Setup

You can print all or part of your presentation; the slides, outline, speaker's notes, and audience handouts, in colour or in black and white and no matter what you print, the process is basically the same. In this section we will learn how we can:

● Select an appropriate output format for slide presentation; overhead, handout, 35mm slides, on-screen show.
● Change slide orientation for either landscape or portrait.

Exercise 5.1

For this exercise we will return to using our Buying a House presentation.

1. Open the presentation House.ppt and make sure that you are positioned on slide one.

2. The first thing we have to do is tell PowerPoint what it is we want to print. You do this by clicking on the option **File I Page Setup...** on the Menu Bar and the dialogue window shown in Figure 5.1 will appear.

Figure 5.1 Setting up the page format before printing.

3. Here we can use the **Slides sized for:** drop down list to select the type of printout we want. In the example shown in Figure 5.2 we have selected **A4 size paper**.

Figure 5.2 Selecting the output media.

4. On the right hand side of the **Page Setup** dialogue window there is a section headed **Orientation** as in Figure 5.3 Here we can select whether to print our slides in either **Portrait** or **Landscape** mode. Similarly we can instruct PowerPoint to print our Notes, Handouts, or Outline in either **Portrait** or **Landscape** layout.

Figure 5.3 Determining the orientation.

5. Once you are happy with your Page Setup settings just click on **OK** to accept them and when you subsequently print your presentation these values will be used.

Summary

In this section we have seen how you simply open the presentation you want to print and choose whether you wish to print slides, handouts, notes pages, or an outline on the Page Setup dialogue window. Also, you specify the orientation of the printed output.

5.2. Prepare for Distribution

Before we actually print our presentation we might want to consider whether we need to provide additional information to aid the presenter and ensure that there are no obvious typos or spelling errors which might spoil our presentation. Therefore, in this section we will see how we can:

● Add notes to slides for the presenter.
● Number the slides.
● Use the spell-check program and make changes where necessary.

Exercise 5.2

For this exercise we will once again use our Buying a House presentation.

step **1.** If it is not already open, open the presentation House.ppt and make sure that you are positioned on slide one.

step **2.** To add notes for the presenter to our slides click on the **Notes Page View** button and the display will change so that the current slide is at the top with a text box area for adding notes underneath, like in Figure 5.4.

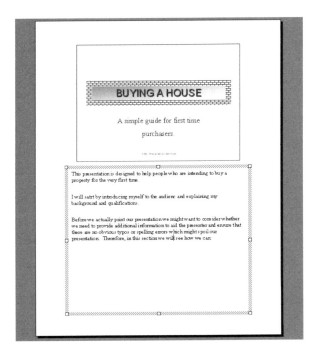

Figure 5.4 Adding Notes to a slide.

step **3.** As well as adding notes for the presenter we might want to automatically number the slides for easy reference. We can do this very simply by selecting **View | Header and Footer...** on the Menu Bar and the tabbed dialogue window as shown in Figure 5.5 will appear:

Figure 5.5 Defining Header and Footer information.

4. On the **Slide** tab of this window you can specify whether you want to include the Date and Time, Slide number, and Footer on either a single slide by clicking on the **Apply** button or on all slides in the presentation by clicking on the **Apply to All** button. Note that the second tab **Notes and Handouts** allows you to specify the same settings for these views.

> **You can also specify whether or not things like the date and time, footer, and slide numbers appear on ALL slides by editing the Slide Master as described previously.**

5. Finally, before we actually print our presentation we need to check whether there are any spelling mistakes or typos which could detract from a professional looking piece of work. To check the spelling click on the **Spelling** icon on the **Standard** Toolbar or select **Tools | Spelling...** on the Menu Bar. This will start the Spelling Check and if any misspelt words are found then the window shown in Figure 5.6 will appear:

Figure 5.6 The Spelling Check has found what it thinks is a misspelt word.

6. Here we can either accept any of the suggested spellings by clicking on the **Change** or **Change All** buttons, type in our own word(s) in the **Change to:** box, ignore the misspelt word by clicking on the **Ignore** or **Ignore All** buttons, and add the word to the CUSTOM.DIC (dictionary) by clicking on the **Add** button.

7. After the whole presentation has been checked for spelling errors the box shown in Figure 5.7 will appear and you can just click on **OK** to return to your presentation.

Figure 5.7 The end of the Spelling Check.

information

PowerPoint can be set to check your spelling as you actually type any text. If you select Tools I Options... and click on the Spelling tab you can turn this feature on or off. When active any words which the Spelling Check thinks are misspelt are highlighted with a squiggly red line.

shortcut

Rather than checking the spelling for an entire presentation you can constrain the check by selecting an area of text first.

Summary

In this section we have seen how we can provide aids to the presenter by adding speaker notes and numbering the slides in a presentation. We have also looked at using the Spelling check facilities to identify and correct any misspelt words in our presentation. Using these facilities should help to ensure that our presentation is as accurate and professional looking as possible.

5.3. Printing

Before we commit our presentation to paper we may need to preview the output to make sure what we are printing is exactly what we require (basically you should preview a printout so that you don't waste reams of paper printing the presentation in the wrong format or layout). Therefore in this section we will learn how to:

● Preview the presentation document in slide, outline, slide sorter, or notes view.

● Print slides in various views and output formats.

Exercise 5.3

For this exercise we will once again use our Buying a House presentation.

1. If it is not already open, open the presentation House.ppt and make sure that you are positioned on slide one.

2. You can preview the different types of printouts by selecting the appropriate view using the view control buttons situated in the bottom left hand corner of the main window.

3. To print a presentation using a certain layout click on the **File | Print...** option on the Menu Bar. This then allows you to select various printing options as shown in Figure 5.8.

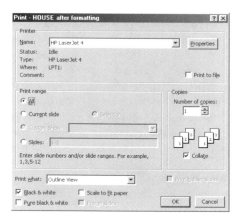

Figure 5.8 Controlling the printing of a presentation.

4. This is quite a complicated dialogue box with numerous options so we need to examine it in detail. At the top is the **Printer** area where you can select which printer you wish to use. This will always display the current Windows default printer but you can change it if you wish using the drop down list. The **Print range** area allows you to specify which parts of the presentation you want to print. For example, you can select All, Current slide, currently selected slides, a custom show, or specific ranges of slides. In the **Copies** area you can set the number of copies to be printed and whether the printed pages are to be collated or not. Lastly, at the bottom there is a **Print what:** box with a drop down list where you can select what you want to print, as in Figure 5.9.

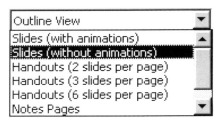

Figure 5.9 Selecting what you want to print.

5. Once you have made your choices simply click on the **OK** button to start the printing process. You may need to experiment with the various options available for printing so that you become familiar with the type of printouts that PowerPoint can produce.

information

If you print from the Slide Sorter View you would probably expect PowerPoint to print a set of miniature slides. However, this does not happen and instead whatever type of print that is selected in the Print what: box will be printed. The same goes when printing from other displayed views. To print a set of small slides you need to select Handouts (2 slides per page), Handouts (3 slides per page), or Handouts (6 slides per page) as required.

Summary

In this section we have seen that there are numerous different ways that you can print information from your presentations. Although PowerPoint doesn't have a Print Preview option which other Microsoft Office applications like Word and Excel have, you can get an idea

what your printout will look like by selecting the appropriate display view. The only area where you might have difficulty is when printing miniature slides so you must remember to use the audience handouts printing option so that you can print two, three, or six slides on a page.

Review Questions

1. What procedure would you use to print audience handouts in landscape format?

2. Which view would you use to add presenter notes to the slides in a presentation?

3. How could you easily number every slide in a presentation?

4. If a presentation contains 20 slides how could you check the spelling on just the first 5?

5. How can you instruct PowerPoint to print on a particular printer?

6. You need 10 copies of your audience handouts but you don't have access to a photocopier. How can you easily produce these?

6

Slide Show Effects

In this chapter you will learn how to

- *Add pre-set animation effects to slides.*
- *Change pre-set animation effects.*
- *Add slide transition effects.*

So far we have only seen the basic Slide Show facilities which can be used to display our presentations in a simple sequence of slides. However, PowerPoint has some very flexible animation features which we can use to make our slide shows much more dynamic and appealing.

6.1. Pre-set Animation

One technique that we can use to liven up our presentations is to apply movement or animation to certain elements of our slides. Therefore, in this section we will see how we can:

● Add pre-set animation effects to slides.
● Change pre-set animation effects.

Exercise 6.1

For this exercise we will once again use our Buying a House presentation.

1. If it is not already open, open the presentation House.ppt and make sure that you are positioned on slide one. Your first slide should look something like Figure 6.1 but don't worry if it isn't exactly the same, so long as it is roughly similar.

Figure 6.1 Slide one should look similar to this.

2. First of all we will start off by animating the Title at the top of the slide so click on it once to select it. Next, select **Slide Show | Preset Animation** from the Menu Bar and you will see a list of options as in Figure 6.2.

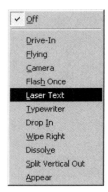

Figure 6.2 Animation options.

step **3.** Click on one to select it and the menu will disappear. At first sight nothing seems to have changed but if we now click on the **Slide Show | Animation Preview** option on the Menu Bar a small preview window should open up as in Figure 6.3 showing us what the animation effect will do to the slide when we run the normal Slide Show.

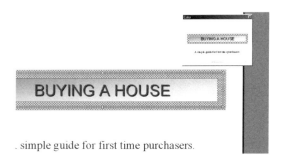

Figure 6.3 The Animation Preview window.

step **4.** We can also apply animation effects to other elements on a slide and in fact any object can be animated simply by selecting it and using the **Slide Show | Animation Preview** option on the Menu Bar. Try out the various animations available to see what they do and use the **Preview Animation** option to see the effect in action.

step **5.** Whilst the Preset Animation effects can be used to enhance a Slide Show we can also tailor animation effects to produce a greater variety of effects. To do this select **Slide Show | Custom Animation...** on the Menu Bar and the dialogue window shown in Figure 6.4 will appear:

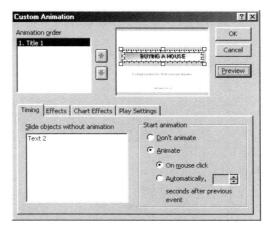

Figure 6.4 Creating a Custom Animation.

6. On the **Timing** tab we can decide what event triggers an animation effect. For example, it might be automatic when the slide is displayed, when you click with the mouse during a Slide Show, or after a number of seconds following the previous event.

7. Clicking on the **Effects** tab displays another series of options as in Figure 6.5 where we can select exactly how a particular animation effect should work.

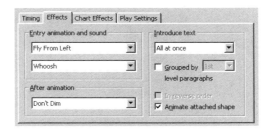

Figure 6.5 Further options for controlling animations.

8. Here you can select different types of sub effects using the **Entry animation and sound** control settings in the relevant drop down lists. There are lots of options for entry animation and once again it is best to try a few out to see what they do. You can preview them by clicking on the **Preview** button. Also on the **Effects** tab you can alter the way that text appears during an animation by accessing the drop down list under the **Introduce text** heading.

9. When you are satisfied with your changes click on the OK button to make them active in your Slide Show.

Summary

By using the PowerPoint animation features you can really add some "pizzazz" to your presentations. As we have seen in this section there are numerous options and combinations of effects to play with and it can be easy to get distracted by the animation effects available.

6.2. Transitions

Not only can you animate objects on individual slides but PowerPoint also allows you to define how the changes between separate slides take place. These are known as slide transitions and in this section we will explore the options available to:

● Add slide transition effects.

Exercise 6.2

For this exercise we will once again use our Buying a House presentation.

1. If it is not already open, open the presentation House.ppt and make sure that you are positioned on slide one.

2. Next select the option **Slide Show I Slide Transition** from the Menu Bar and the dialogue window shown in Figure 6.6 should appear.

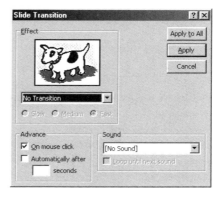

Figure 6.6 Selecting a slide transition option.

3. Here a drop down list allows you to select different transition effects. As you select an effect the small graphic above shows you exactly how it will appear in your slide show. Once you have decided which transition effect you want to use you can either use the same effect between all the slides in the presentation by clicking on the **Apply to All** button or restrict the transition effect to appear only between the current slide and the next one in the sequence. Notice that you can also decide whether slides appear on mouse click or automatically after a specific number of seconds. Lastly, you can apply a sound to the transition and specify whether it should play just once or loop until the next transition.

4. Use the **Slide Show I View Show** option from the Menu Bar to check through the various slide transitions and if you are not happy go back and re-set them using the procedures above.

Summary

In this section we have seen how we can set up different types of transitions between slides and control how the changing of slides can be triggered. Once again it is best to try out various transition effects to see which ones work best for your particular presentation.

Review Questions

1. There are two different ways that you can add movement to a presentation, What are they?

2. When animating an object on a slide how can you see the effect without actually running the Slide Show?

3. If a preset animation doesn't do exactly what you want, what can you do?

4. How can you alter the way that text appears during an animation?

5. How can you ensure that a particular slide transition appears between every slide in a presentation?

6. What is the best way to ensure that all slide transitions are working as you intended?

View a
Slide Show

In this chapter you will learn how to

- *Commence and conclude a slide show on any selected slide.*

- *Use on-screen navigation tools.*

- *Hide a slide or group of slides so that they do not display during a slide show.*

Now that we have done all the hard work in creating, editing and enhancing our presentation it is time to learn how to use PowerPoint to manage the delivery of the presentation.

7.1. Delivering a Presentation

PowerPoint has several different tools that we can use to prepare a presentation for showing to an audience. In this section we will see how we can:

● Start a slide show on any slide.
● Use on-screen navigation tools.
● Hide slides.

Exercise 7.1

For this exercise we will once again use our Buying a House presentation.

1. If it is not already open, open the presentation House.ppt and make sure that you are positioned on slide one.

2. When you start a slide show by selecting **Slide Show I View Show** on the Menu Bar PowerPoint will display each slide in sequence starting at the first slide in the presentation by default. However, you can control precisely the range of slides to be displayed by selecting the **Slide Show I Set Up Show...** option on the Menu Bar which will display the dialogue box shown in Figure 7.1.

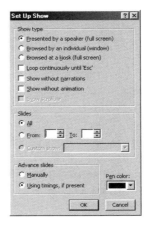

Figure 7.1 Setting up a Slide Show.

step**3.** Here you can choose the Show type, specify the start and end slides, and decide whether slides should change manually or after preset timings. Remember that timings between slides can be set using the slide transition options described in the previous exercise.

When running a Slide Show in manual advance mode you can either click once with the mouse or press the space bar on the keyboard to move to the next slide in the sequence. You can also use the Page Up | Page Down or cursor up | cursor down arrow keys to move forwards and backwards one slide at a time through the slide sequence. To stop the Slide Show at any time press the Esc key on the keyboard. If you press the F1 key during a Slide Show than a list of controls appears.

step**4.** When you run a Slide Show if you move the mouse slightly you may notice a small icon appear on the slide in the bottom left hand corner which looks like this.

Clicking on this icon with the mouse causes a small shortcut menu to appear on-screen as in Figure 7.2.

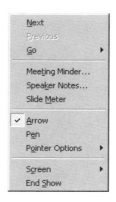

Figure 7.2 The shortcut pop-up menu.

step**5.** If you point to **Go** and then select **Slide Navigator** a window like that shown in Figure 7.3 will appear:

Figure 7.3 Using the Slide Navigator to Go To a slide.

6. Here you can select any slide in your presentation to move to next when you press the **Go To** button.

7. Running the standard Slide Show gives us rather limited facilities to control the displaying of slides but fortunately PowerPoint has another trick up its sleeve in the form of on-screen navigation tools. These are called Action Buttons which can be placed anywhere on a slide and will allow the presenter to move quickly and easily to any point in the Slide Show simply by clicking on the relevant control buttons with the mouse. Figure 7.4 shows the Action Buttons available.

Figure 7.4 Selecting an Action Button for use on a slide.

8. Action Buttons can be set to appear on any slide in a presentation by selecting **Slide Show | Action Buttons** on the Menu Bar and then choosing a button to be inserted on the slide. At this point a dialogue box like that in Figure 7.5 will appear asking you to confirm the action which will be associated with this button.

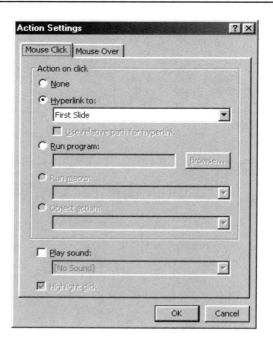

Figure 7.5 Defining the action to be triggered by an Action Button.

step **9.** Normally you will just want to accept the default action so simply click on **OK** to confirm this.

step **10.** Once inserted on a slide an Action Button can be moved, resized and formatted just like any other AutoShape. You decide which and how many Action Buttons you want to appear on your slides. For example, you might want to include the Action Buttons shown in Figure 7.6 on your slides:

Figure 7.6 Examples of Action Buttons.

caution!

Different sets of Action Buttons can be placed on individual slides within a presentation but if you want the same Action Buttons to appear on ALL your slides simply place them on the Slide Master.

11. Occasionally you might want to 'hide' a slide or a group of slides so that they do not display during a Slide Show. You can do this from the Slide View screen by selecting **Slide Show I Hide Slide** from the Menu Bar which will hide the current slide as shown in Figure 7.7.

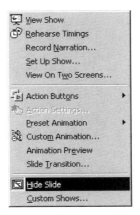

Figure 7.7 Hiding a slide.

12. Unfortunately in Slide View you don't get any indication that a slide is hidden and therefore you need to select the **Slide Sorter View** which shows any hidden slides with a diagonal line through the slide number, as in Figure 7.8.

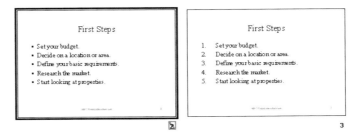

Figure 7.8 Slide Sorter View showing a hidden slide on the left.

13. Also on the **Slide Sorter View** you can select multiple slides by holding down the Shift key on the keyboard whilst clicking on slides with the mouse. Once multiple slides have been selected you can hide them by selecting **Slide Show I Hide Slide** from the Menu Bar.

14. During a Slide Show if you need to display a hidden slide you must position yourself at the slide immediately preceding the hidden one and then click on the shortcut menu icon and select **Go I Hidden Slide**. Alternatively, you can click on the shortcut menu icon on any slide in a presentation, point to **Go**, click **Slide Navigator**, and then double-click the slide you want. Numbers in parentheses designate hidden slides as shown in Figure 7.9.

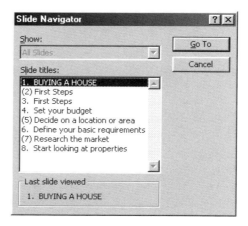

Figure 7.9 Slide Navigator showing hidden slide with numbers in brackets.

If you opt to reveal a hidden slide during a Slide Show it then remains revealed for the duration of that show, so if you move backwards and forwards you will see it. However, re-running the Slide Show will cause any slides marked for hiding to be hidden once more.

Summary

In this section we have seen that there are numerous ways in which we can control and manage the presentation of a Slide Show either by specifying a range of slides to display, navigating through the sequence of slides, and temporarily hiding slides so that they are not displayed.

As usual you are advised to experiment and play around with these various options so that you become familiar with their capabilities and how they work.

Review Questions

1. How can you make a Slide Show start on a particular slide?

2. How can you make a Slide Show end on a particular slide?

3. What happens if you click on the navigation icon during a Slide Show?

4. What are Action Buttons and how are they used?

5. How can you tell whether a slide is hidden or not?

6. How can you display a hidden slide in the middle of a Slide Show?

Final Summary

Now that you have reached the end of this guide you should have gained a good insight into the principles of using PowerPoint. However, this guide is not intended to be a fully comprehensive training manual for PowerPoint 97 and there are many aspects of the package which have not been covered. Therefore, you are encouraged to further explore the capabilities and features of PowerPoint in order to broaden your knowledge of the software.

If you have access to the Internet then you should start by visiting the Microsoft PowerPoint web site where you will find plenty of additional information about the product.

http://www.microsoft.com/office/powerpoint/default.htm

If you don't have access to the Internet or if you are happier learning from a book there are numerous published training guides for PowerPoint covering every single facet of using the software.

Index

European Computer Driving Licence™

the european pc skills standard

★ ★ ★ ®
★ ★
★ ECDL ★
★ ★
★ ★

Springer's study guides have been designed to complement the ECDL syllabus, and be consistent with the content contained within it. Each study guide enables you to successfully complete the European Driving Licence (ECDL). The books cover a range of specific knowledge areas and skill sets, with clearly defined learning objectives, broken down into seven modules.

Each module has been written in clear, jargon-free language, with self-paced exercises and regular review questions, to help prepare you for ECDL Tests.

Titles in the series include:

- **Module 1: Basic Concepts of Information Technology**
  ISBN: 1-85233-442-8   Softcover   £9.95

- **Module 2: Using the Computer & Managing Files**
  ISBN: 1-85233-443-6   Softcover   £9.95

- **Module 3: Word Processing**
  ISBN: 1-85233-444-4   Softcover   £9.95

- **Module 4: Spreadsheets**
  ISBN: 1-85233-445-2   Softcover   £9.95

- **Module 5: Database**
  ISBN: 1-85233-446-0   Softcover   £9.95

- **Module 6: Presentation**
  ISBN: 1-85233-447-9   Softcover   £9.95

- **Module 7: Information & Communication**
  ISBN: 1-85233-448-7   Softcover   £9.95

All books are available, of course, from all good booksellers (who can order them even if they are not in stock), but if you have difficulties you can contact the publisher direct by telephoning +44 (0) 1483 418822 or by emailing orders@svl.co.uk

For details of other Springer books and journals, please visit

www.springer.de

Accessible Access

Mark Whitehorn and Bill Marklyn

Accessible Access 2000 assumes that you start with no knowledge of Access or databases and takes you to the point where you can create and use a multi-table database.

> *"These two authors make a perfect team. Bill Marklyn knows the product inside out and Mark Whitehorn makes the information accessible."*
> Neil Fawcett, Group Technical Editor,
> VNU BUSINESS PUBLICATIONS

> *"PCW and Amazon.co.uk contributor Mark Whitehorn is that rare combination—an expert in his field, databases, and a fine writer too, with a talent for honing a complex subject down to its essentials."*
> Tamsin Todd - Computers & Internet Editor,
> AMAZON.CO.UK

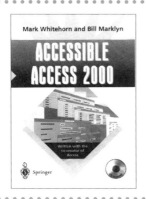

All books are available, of course, from all good booksellers (who can order them even if they are not in stock), but if you have difficulties you can contact the publisher direct by telephoning +44 (0) 1483 418822 or by emailing orders@svl.co.uk

June 2000 ● Softcover ● 318 pages ● ISBN: 1-85233-313-8 ● £24.50